Women WHO PUSH THE LIMITS

PRESENTS

7 KEYS TO IMPROVING YOUR CUSTOMER SERVICE

Lynn W. Murphy, M.Ed.

Flint Hills Publishing

Women Who Push the Limits Presents
7 Keys to Improving Your
Customer Service

Cover Design by Amy Albright

Flint Hills Publishing
www.flinthillspublishing.com

Printed in the U.S.A.

ISBN: 978-1-953583-10-9

Library of Congress Application Pending

DEDICATION

To Norma and Bob, my amazing parents, who taught me, early in life, the fine art of serving others and the importance of enjoying life no matter how hard you have to work.

Table of Contents

Introduction   1

Key 1: Focus on Your Customer   13

Key 2: Serving Your Customer is
Everyone's Job   17

Key 3: Treat Your Customers the
Way THEY Want to be Treated   23

Key 4: Use Your Customer's Name   29

Key 5: Tell Your Customer What You
Can Do, Not What You Can't   33

Key 6: Sincerely Apologize When
Things Go Wrong   37

Key 7: Value Customer Complaints   45

Final Thoughts   51

References   53

About the Author   55

INTRODUCTION

I must have inherited the customer service gene from my parents. Growing up during the 1950s in a small motel my parents owned and operated in Tucson, Arizona, the importance of serving our guests well was ingrained in me from the time I was three years old.

Nobody explained to me that these guests were the ones who made it possible to have food on our table and clothes in our closets. But my parents' attention to every detail of the guests' experiences demonstrated how essential the guests were.

My mother, and sometimes another maid when the motel was busy and she could afford to hire someone, made sure the rooms were spotless and comfortable. The pool was sparkling. The patio was welcoming with its comfortable chairs and tables where guests could enjoy conversation or solitude in the sunny Tucson weather. The verdant lawn, towering date palms, and beautiful rose garden were tended with care by my father.

A postcard of my parents' motel, 1954.

There was no such thing as office hours or weekends off. If a guest wanted to check in at midnight or check out in the early morning hours, my parents served them with a friendly smile. Guests awoke on Christmas Day to find a holiday stocking filled with my mother's homemade cookies hanging from their door. They were *guests* in the true sense of the word.

Even as my younger sister and I engaged in childhood enterprises and energetic adventures around the motel, we were expected to put the guests first. At an early age, I understood I must be polite, helpful, and respectful, especially to our guests.

Different guests came and went. Some we never saw again. Others became family friends. Twice we were excited to have a movie star as a guest. If you're of my generation, you may remember Donna Reed and Richard Widmark. Under the glass on the front counter, my dad proudly displayed snapshots of these stars lounging by the pool. No matter who the person was, whether they were there for a night, a week, or a month, my parents treated each one as a welcomed visitor. Providing the best possible experience for each guest was our family's way of life 24 hours a day, 7 days a week, 365 days a year.

This postcard features my family (that's me on my dad's lap near the edge of the pool) and guests, also in 1954.

My parents' brand of customer-focused service nurtured relationships with our guests that brought many of them back year after year.

The winter sunshine beckoned a retired couple from Oklahoma every winter. The grandmotherly Mrs. Hancock loved to treat us girls to lunch at an upscale restaurant. Then, to our delight, she gave us each a dollar to spend on anything we wanted at the variety store. The special perfume in crystal bottles and velvet bags she sent us every Christmas made us feel so very grown-up. This family friendship lasted for years, even after we moved out of the motel when I was a teen.

The outgoing, fun-loving DiGrazias escaped New York winters, heading to our motel every year. Mr. D. indulged my sister and me, laughing at our splashy games and water balloon fights in the pool. On those balmy evenings when guests gathered around the patio for cookouts, he grilled his secret chicken recipe. Thoughts of the pungent smell of garlic and rosemary marinade and the taste of the crispy charcoal crust still make my mouth water.

Ina drove her red convertible Volkswagen bug from Massachusetts for her annual weeks-long Tucson vacation. She became my mother's friend and was our fun and tolerant playmate. She let us think it was a privilege that she allowed us to gleefully bail water out of her car when she left the top down in the rain.

That customer service gene fully blossomed during my childhood. I internalized the value of building warm relationships with guests and treating them like family. It's part of who I am today so many decades later. It's automatic—part of my DNA.

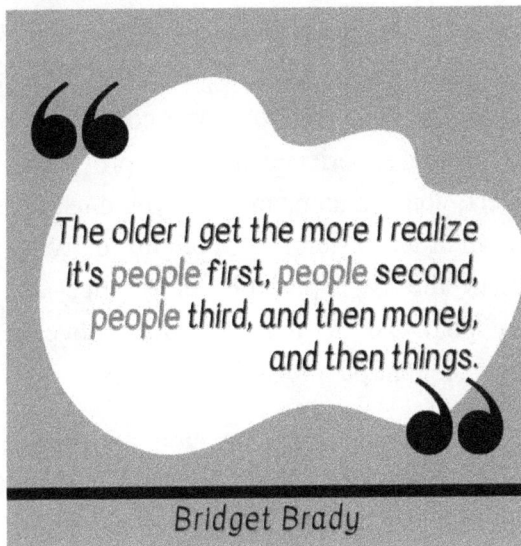

> 66
>
> The older I get the more I realize it's people first, people second, people third, and then money, and then things.
> 99
>
> Bridget Brady

So, it was no surprise to me that many of the women I interviewed for my project, *Women Who Push the Limits*, expressed a strong commitment to serving others whether through their business or community service. This commitment to exceptional service is a fundamental part of what makes women successful in business and life. **Some of their ideas, along with my own, are woven throughout these powerful customer service principles that I'm sharing with you here. . .**

Regardless of the business you're in, you're in the CUSTOMER SERVICE BUSINESS. If you're not serving your customers, and serving them well, you're engaged in a hobby, not a business.

Customer service must be your top priority. When you consider that the majority of businesses (some studies say as many as 90%) are competing based mainly on the experience they are providing their customers, you'll understand why you must focus on service. In order to stand out, commit to giving your customers the best possible experience as your primary goal. To do that you must develop and sharpen excellent people skills.

When you and your team develop these skills and demonstrate passion for offering unparalleled customer service, you'll have loyal customers who are happy to give you their money, rave about you to their friends and family, and post positive business-generating reviews on social media.

How important is customer service? The Microsoft 2017 State of Global Customer Service Report declares that customer experience is the "engine that drives wallet share, brand loyalty, and the **future of your business**." Many comprehensive long-term studies reinforce the importance of offering unrivaled customer service in establishing and growing a successful business.

When you look at the statistics, you'll recognize the financial advantages of providing outstanding customer experiences. Companies that focus on their customers are 60% more profitable than companies that don't. Customers are willing to pay significantly more for an exceptional experience. (A 2021 survey of over 1,900 business professionals by SuperOffice puts this number at 86%.)

Companies are losing billions of dollars a year due to inferior customer service. Don't be one of them.

Research by Peppers & Rogers Group reveals when people quit doing business with a company, 60% do so because of poor customer service. They leave when they believe they were treated with indifference by an employee or when they felt unappreciated. A much lower percentage of customers who left a business did so because of dissatisfaction with a product, finding a better price elsewhere, or because they were enticed away by the competition.

On the other hand, almost every customer who believes they had a great experience with your company will make another purchase from you.

Personal connections have become even more important as the world deals with the pandemic and people are feeling isolated. *Zendesks Customer Experience Trends 2020* reports half of customers surveyed say the experience they have with a company is more important now than ever. These customers would switch to a competitor if they had even **one** negative experience with a company.

If you've been relying on low price points to grow your business, you may be surprised to know that merely offering the lowest prices is not a guarantee of success. Consider the department retailer Nordstrom that charges premium prices but delivers some of the most exceptional service of any business. Nordstrom has built their reputation upon their culture of customer service. More than 70% of purchasers report that their customer experience is more important than the price they pay.

Empathy is the ability to identify with the feelings, thoughts, or attitudes of others. Empathy is an essential metric for measuring customer experiences, especially as we've been more isolated during the pandemic. Buyers want representatives to be empathetic; they want to do business with companies that share their values, such as diversity and inclusion.

Unleash your creative woman-in-business persona. Put your own unique stamp on the service you deliver. Do something special and unexpected to stand out from the competition.

When I place an online order for an item, I just hope the item turns out to be as it has been represented, is decent quality, and hasn't been damaged in shipment. I expect whoever ships the item to throw it in a box or a bag with nothing more than an order slip. So, I was pleasantly surprised when I received my order from a catalog company I had never done business with before. The item wasn't expensive, but the company packaged it as if it were priceless. The item was carefully protected in several layers of tissue with another layer of tissue neatly folded and tucked around the item. A handwritten note was taped to the tissue with a bright gold sticker. The note included my name, thanked me for my purchase, and wished me much enjoyment from the item. To my amazement, it was signed by a real person. Knowing that someone took the time to handle my purchase with such care and attention made me feel truly valued. I continue to order from that company and enjoy their personal attention as well as their products.

Polish your natural ability to practice empathy and add a unique personal touch to your service. Show that extra attention to detail. What would surprise and delight you if you were the customer? Then do that and surprise and delight your customer. You'll be a customer service-star as you watch your business skyrocket.

Make your customers' experience easy and pleasant whether you're interacting with them in person, on the phone, on your website, or on their mobile devices. Put yourself in your customer's shoes. Listen carefully to their feedback and make changes to improve their experience.

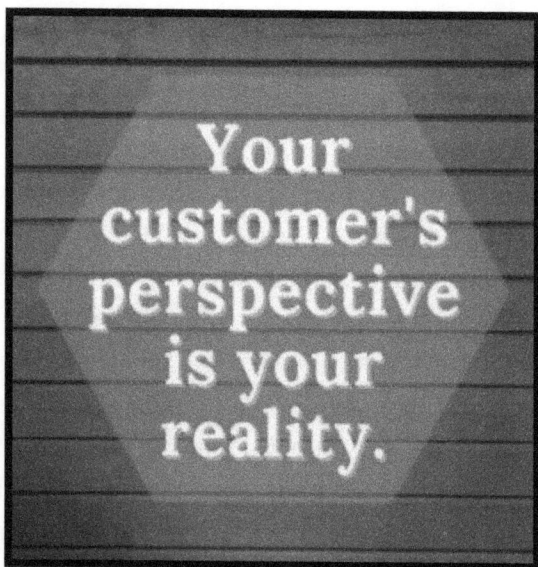

Your customer's perspective is your reality.

Delivering an incomparable customer experience is the cornerstone of creating a successful, resilient, and profitable business. It's your customers' opinion of how they feel they've been treated, not yours, that counts. Their perceptions of your service will influence their loyalty and what they say to others about you and your business. If they like you and feel valued, they will continue doing business with you. They'll write those glowing online reviews. Their referrals to their friends will help you grow your business.

I use the word *customer* to refer to the person whom you serve. Different businesses use the words *client* or *guest* or *patient*. Substitute whatever you prefer to call the people who pay you for what you provide. Regardless of the term you use, your exceptional treatment of them will ensure they keep coming back and that they will increase your business by recommending it to others.

In this book, you'll find **seven keys to delivering high quality, customer-focused service that will ensure your business success** when you implement them in your business. As you study these keys, think about how you can apply them to your business and your team. Notice the areas where you are doing well and where you can improve. These tips are simple yet powerful. Implement them immediately to push the limits of excellence and improve your customer service. Watch as you ignite your business prosperity.

Here's to your continued success!

Lynn

> **"**
> Customer service is the experience
> we deliver to our customer.
> It's the promise we keep to
> the customer.
> It's how we follow through for
> the customer.
> It's how we make them feel when
> they do business with us.
>
> **SHEP HYKEN**

#1

FOCUS ON YOUR CUSTOMER

Focus on your customer. This may seem an obvious statement, but it's more difficult to put the concept into practice.

Here's a question I ask clients in my workshops: Who do you work for? As a woman who pushes limits, you're an entrepreneur, a business owner, a solopreneur—or that's your dream—so you may answer that you work for yourself or your family. If you're still drawing a paycheck, you may say you work for your boss, manager, supervisor, or the business owner.

While each of those responses contains a morsel of truth, the best answer is that **you work for your customers**. Unless you are printing counterfeit money in the back room of your office, it is your customers' money that keeps the doors open, pays the expenses, and determines whether your business will survive and thrive. Never forget, that's who you work for.

Back in the Dark Ages when mobile phones were first introduced, I was selling commercial real estate and was often driving around town for hours at a time. It's hard to imagine now what it was like not to be able to communicate with clients and prospects immediately. Investing a couple thousand dollars in a phone that was hard-wired into the car seemed like a good investment. (Yes, those first-generation mobile phones did cost that much!) There were no phone stores at that time, only sales representatives who met prospects in person. The young man who showed up at my office to sell me a phone was not focused on me. He was focused on his script. In order to convince me to spend that much money on this new "gadget," he launched into his memorized speech. *How much did I spend on calls from pay phones every month?* (Does anyone remember when there was a pay phone on every corner?) *How inconvenient was it for me to have to keep change on hand for the pay phones? Was I comfortable having to jump out of my car in all kinds of weather and stand at a pay phone with noisy traffic going by?* I rarely used a pay phone. No, I didn't have change rattling around in my car so I could deposit a quarter every time I wanted to make a call. When his scripted approach didn't get me excited about investing in a car phone, he moved on to the next item on his script—another question that didn't apply to me. *How much did I want to pay each month on a payment plan?* I didn't need or want a payment plan. Did the script writer assume everyone wanted a payment plan, or just women?

None of his scripted questions applied to me. He could have saved himself a lot of time and me a lot of frustration if he'd asked me what I wanted to know and what my questions were. He would have recognized, a few minutes into our very awkward conversation, that I was ready to purchase the phone for cash. My questions were about the equipment, installation, and scheduling. I wonder if he ever learned to focus on his customer's wants and needs instead of on his script. Or if his sales career was short-lived.

Numerous studies across decades agree that the companies with the highest market share, profitability, revenue growth, and customer satisfaction are the ones that are customer-focused. In his 2019 article, *The ROI of Customer Experience [Facts, Figures, Tips & More],* Matthew DeCarlo cites recent studies and reports by well-known market research companies and management consulting firms attesting to the benefits of focusing on your customers. The statistics quoted in the article confirm the significant positive return on investment of this customer-centered focus.

Companies ranking highest in customer satisfaction

outperformed their competition.

- They averaged 17% growth over five years while companies with poor customer satisfaction scores averaged just 3% growth.
- They grew their revenues 4% to 8% above their competitors.
- They retained loyal customers who spend as much as 7 times more and stay longer than companies with only average customer satisfaction scores.

Just knowing you need to be customer-focused is not enough. It is essential that you create a clear vision that drives business practices, then train everyone who works for you to implement those practices. When your organizational culture is focused on your customers, you'll be delighted that the results show up in your bottom line.

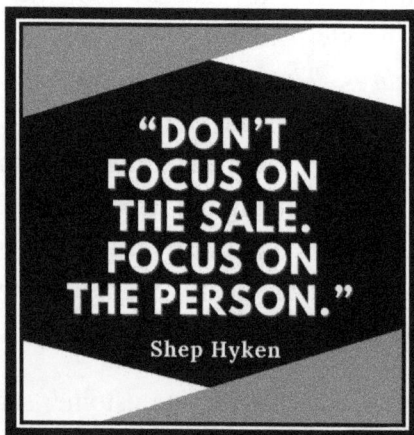

> **"DON'T FOCUS ON THE SALE. FOCUS ON THE PERSON."**
>
> Shep Hyken

#2

SERVING YOUR CUSTOMERS IS EVERYONE'S JOB

Every person in your organization, regardless of the department they're in or the role they play, is an integral part of your Customer Service Department. As a successful businesswoman, you must be committed to making this a reality.

If you or members of your team are not operating with that commitment, you can be sure your *Sales Prevention Department* is actively, though surreptitiously, damaging your company's reputation and costing you business. These team members will damage your brand by turning off customers. They will damage morale of others in your organization and make it more difficult for everyone to provide exceptional service to your customers. You may not know why customers fail to return.

You may not even recognize that you are losing them until you notice the red ink on the bottom line. If you notice this, survey your customers to see how they perceive their experience with you and your business.

Immediately identify anyone who is lurking in your *Sales Prevention Department*. Coach them, train them, or replace them as fast as you can if they don't embody your customer-focused philosophy.

I live near a local market that offers premium grocery items as well as hot and cold deli options, mouthwatering Italian entrees, and scrumptious freshly-prepared meals. Pre-COVID, my husband and I didn't take time to cook on a regular basis, so we shopped at this market regularly. Their high-quality products (and high-quality prices) are usually accompanied by high-quality service. So, I was shocked by my experience when I asked an employee to help me find a product I didn't usually purchase.

This young woman in her store uniform approached me from the opposite direction as I was unsuccessfully searching the aisles. When I asked her where I could find the apple juice, she replied, "I don't know; I'm new here." Then she just stared at me blankly, apparently waiting for me to say something while making no effort to find someone who wasn't so new and could find the juice for me. I didn't expect an employee of this upscale grocery store to be confused about her customer service responsibilities. I would have expected better training from her employer.

I wandered down another aisle and found a different employee pushing a handcart loaded with boxes. His response was what I expect from the usually well-trained employees. "I have chilled juice in the cold case over there or warm on the shelf. Which would you like? I'll show you where it is." With a smile, he abandoned his cart, accompanied me to the aisle, and made sure I found what I wanted. He gave me no excuses. He made me feel like a very important customer.

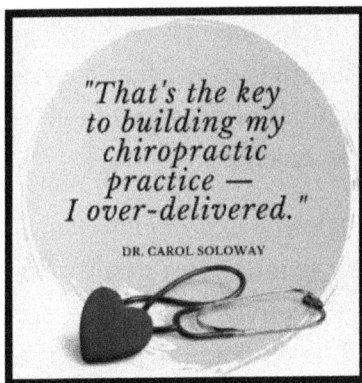

"That's the key to building my chiropractic practice — I over-delivered."

DR. CAROL SOLOWAY

Follow these steps to create a culture in which everyone puts your customers first:

1. Hire people who have a positive attitude and a passionate willingness to serve. Make sure part of your hiring process includes assessing their attitude and dedication to service. Companies like Southwest Airlines make it a priority to hire for attitude and train the skills.

2. Clearly define in writing a bold, audacious vision for a culture where everyone recognizes the importance of serving your external and internal customers. Acknowledge their commitment to delivering your first-class brand of service with precision, skill, and passion.

3. Reinforce that vision frequently in regular discussions with your team about how they are putting this vision into practice. Make these discussions an essential part of every team meeting. Keep that customer focus in the forefront of your operations every day, in every interaction.

4. Share specific expectations and best practices so your team knows exactly how you want them to deliver remarkable service. There should be no doubt that the highest standard

of customer service is **everyone's** top priority.

5. Empower everyone on your team to be responsive to your customers while doing what's right for your organization. Give them latitude to make decisions on the spot that will show your customers how much they are valued.

6. Create specific goals and metrics for customer service and reward the behavior you want to see. What gets rewarded gets repeated.

"Customer service should not be a department. It should be the entire company."

TONY HSIEH. CEO OF ZAPPOS

#3
TREAT YOUR CUSTOMERS THE WAY THEY WANT TO BE TREATED

We all know the Golden Rule says to treat others the way you want to be treated. But when you're serving your customers, it's **not** about you, it's about **THEM**. So, practice the *Platinum Rule* and treat your customers the way **THEY** want to be treated.

Seek to understand what each customer likes, needs, and wants—not what you think they like, need, and want. Don't assume you know. Ask them questions to clarify your understanding. Listen carefully to their answers. You might be surprised by what issues surface.

Notice your customer's behavioral style and adapt your style to theirs. Because people like and trust others who seem to be like them, your customer will feel more comfortable with you if you modify your behavior to more closely match theirs. Are they talkative and have high energy or are they more reserved? Are they interested in every detail of your product or service, or do they only want you to give them the highlights? Are they comfortable being physically close, or do they need lots of personal space to feel relaxed? Do they share personal information and stories, or do they withdraw if you ask personal questions? Do they enjoy humorous banter, or do they prefer to keep it serious?

For years in my workshops, I've taught my clients how to recognize their customer's preferred style of interacting. Understanding interpersonal behavior and learning to recognize someone's behavioral style opens up effective ways of connecting with your customers. Here is an example that illustrates the point:

> **Gina loves her job working with residents** at the retirement community. She treats them all like family. She spends time listening to their stories and laughing with them. Even when she just passes one of the residents in the hallway, she takes a minute to engage them in a bit of conversation. She brings things she remembers about them into the conversations. She makes them feel special, especially when she compliments someone on their outfit. Her outgoing personality and genuine interest in other people make her one of the most popular employees with the residents.

Tom loves his high-pressure job as manager of the IT department at the same retirement community. He works efficiently, analyzing problems, systems, and technology. His days are spent mostly by himself at his computer making sure the systems for this community of several hundred residents and staff run smoothly. When things don't run smoothly, he scrutinizes the issue and fixes the problem as quickly as possible. The residents and staff appreciate his work behind the scenes to keep things working well.

Whenever Gina came to Tom's office looking for help with a computer system, she treated him the same way she treated the residents. Her cheery greeting was followed by questions about Tom's health, his family, his vacation plans, and even compliments on his wardrobe choices. But she didn't get the response she got from the residents. His gruff, get-to-the-point approach annoyed her. *Why is he so mean? He never asks me how I'm doing. He doesn't care about anyone except himself.*

Tom's frustration with Gina matched her annoyance with him. *Why is she wasting my time? I don't want to talk with her about my kids or dog or vacation plans, and especially not about my shirt. I have too much work to do. Why doesn't she just tell me what she needs and leave me alone so I can fix it?*

Gina and Tom made the mistake of treating each other the way they wanted to be treated. Their failure to recognize the other person's behavioral style damaged the relationship between these two coworkers. Knowing that internal customer service is as important as external customer service, they needed to resolve this issue.

When they learned about the different behavioral styles I taught, they were able to see the issues more clearly. Their annoyance and frustration revolved around the differences in their behavioral preferences and around each expecting the other to treat them the way they wanted to be treated. It wasn't that Tom didn't care about Gina as a person. He was just more focused on the tasks he had to do. He wasn't wired to engage in small talk. His style worked for the primary focus of his job—technology. And Gina wasn't trying to waste his time; she was trying to connect on a personal level like she does so successfully with the residents.

Once they were able to look at their differences from that perspective, they were able to work together more easily—and even laugh about those differences. They came up with a compromise. Tom allows Gina to ask him one personal question which he answers with a smile. Some days, he even makes a friendly comment. Then she moves on to asking the IT question she needs help with and gives Tom space to handle it. They quit making the other person wrong when they accepted that they are just different.

We expect other people to operate the way we do. And we treat people the way we want to be treated. Instead, apply the *Platinum Rule*.

Once you recognize your customer's style, you can adapt your behavior to theirs making them more comfortable interacting with you and making them more likely to do business with you.

Don't get stuck on your own point of view or your own behavior style. Figure out how to treat each customer the way they want to be treated.

With more people doing business online, you may find it more challenging to identify your customer's style and connect with them. You can still do it by listening carefully to how they talk or noticing their style in their electronic correspondence. In your marketing copy, include language that speaks to each of the styles: results, detail, relationship, influence, and fun.

When you authentically connect with your customers and treat them the way **they** want to be treated, you'll create a loyal base of fans who come back again and again and who enthusiastically recommend your services to their friends and family.

#4

USE YOUR CUSTOMER'S NAME

Use your customer's name; it's everyone's favorite word. We all love to hear our own name, and we feel more valued as a customer when we do.

You already know how important it is to smile and greet your customers immediately. Even smiling while you're on the phone with your customer is basic customer service.

The practice of also using your customers' names will make you stand out from your competition. It helps you connect with them and makes them feel special. This is a simple and powerful tool which costs nothing but is seldom utilized. Once you train yourself and your staff to do this, it will come easily and naturally.

Research conducted by nationally recognized employment expert Michael Mercer, Ph.D. reveals that, compared to underachievers, high achievers use a person's name one or two more times in each conversation. Using your customer's name helps propel you and your associates into the high-achiever category.

A few years ago, I traveled for work with another trainer who made a point of remembering people's names. Megan always used names when she spoke to servers in restaurants, flight attendants, hotel employees setting up our training rooms, hotel clerks who checked us in, and anyone whose name tag was visible. If their nametag wasn't visible, she asked their name. It was a remarkable skill and one that made a noticeable difference to the person she addressed and the quality of service she received.

Throughout every training, she consistently addressed each of our workshop participants by name. Using their names created a positive learning environment and a stronger connection with our clients.

If you deal with your customers on the phone, ask each their name and what they'd like you to call them. Some people are comfortable with you calling them by their first name. Others may have other preferences. Since you're focusing on how your customer wants to be treated, ask them. Once you have their name, make a note of it, remember it, and use it frequently.

If you're providing medical services, you will have your patient's chart in hand. There's no excuse for not using their name. Introduce yourself and ask them how they want to be addressed. Don't insult your patients by addressing them by phony terms of endearment such as "dear," "honey," "young lady," or "young man." Using your patient's name will show you respect and value them, and that you think of them as an individual, not as a number or a diagnosis.

In certain families and cultures, such as the military or law enforcement, calling someone "ma'am" or "sir" is considered a sign of respect. Outside those cultures, not everyone sees it that way. It makes me feel old when someone calls me "ma'am." A doctor client of mine always calls me "ma'am." Although I know I'm old enough to be his mother, I don't like being reminded of that! I would much prefer he call me Lynn.

There's another reason not to call someone ma'am or sir: you might be mistaken. It's not always easy to tell someone's gender identity. Don't make assumptions based on their name or voice or appearance. Play it safe and use their name.

Connect with your customer by using their name. You'll make a great impression, strengthen that all-important relationship, and gain the success you deserve.

#5
TELL YOUR CUSTOMERS WHAT YOU CAN DO, NOT WHAT YOU CAN'T

Your customers don't want to hear what you **can't** do. That puts them on the defensive and sets up an argument. Instead, with a helpful attitude tell them what you **can** do for them. Help them see how different solutions could benefit them.

Remember that your interaction with your customers should be focused on **their** needs and wants. Offer options. Make sure those options work for them as well as for you and your business.

Never, never, never tell your customers that something is company policy. (Did I use "never" enough times to make my point?) "Company policy" means nothing to them and will annoy them even more. It's the equivalent of a parent saying, "Because I said so."

> "CUSTOMERS DON'T CARE ABOUT YOUR POLICY, THEY CARE ABOUT ACTION."
>
> *Flavio Martins, Best-Selling Author*

International speaker and best-selling author Larry Winget tells a story of how he experienced the ridiculous imposition of company policies. Late one night, he arrived at a hotel that offers chocolate chip cookies to each guest at check-in. Larry couldn't wait to devour his. The guest checking in next to him told the clerk he didn't like chocolate and declined his cookie. That got Larry's attention. He said, "I'd love to have that cookie!" The clerk refused to give him that second cookie because the company policy was one-cookie-per-guest. Larry argued that the other guest didn't want his, so what was the harm? The other guest agreed. The clerk wouldn't give Larry the cookie because it was already *assigned* to the other guest. (Did they really give each cookie a room assignment? What was going to happen to this poor, unclaimed cookie if Larry didn't take it?) The other guest then asked the clerk for his cookie. It was obvious to the clerk he intended to hand to Larry, and she refused to give it to him saying he'd already declined his cookie.

There may have been a good reason for the hotel policy, perhaps to prevent running out of cookies? But the strict application of this policy in this situation made no sense at all. It angered two businessmen who traveled frequently. Larry has shared this story, including the name of the hotel, with hundreds of thousands of people over dozens of years on his speaking tours. Was saving one cookie truly worth the bad publicity? The clerk's behavior was myopic. She couldn't see that flexibility and a morsel of humor was what was called for in this situation. With the inflexibility she demonstrated, she doesn't belong in the customer service business.

If you're inundated with company policies that control what you can and can't do for your customers, take a hard look at what each policy accomplishes. Eliminate those policies that don't support your customer focus.

This is one place you do not want to push limits unless you're pushing in the direction of serving your customers. Train and support your employees to use sound judgment when imposing any remaining policies. Don't be shortsighted. Make sure you and your employees clearly understand and explain the intent of the policy and **how it benefits your customer**. Then tell your customers what you **can** do, not what you can't.

#6
SINCERLEY APOLOGIZE WHEN THINGS GO WRONG

When something goes wrong, and it will, apologize to your customer, even if you don't think it's your fault or the company's fault. The customer may be expecting to have to fight for what they want, or at least to argue with you. A sincere apology can be so unexpected that it disarms most angry customers.

Make your apology sincere. People can tell when you're parroting something you said because you were told to say it, not because you truly mean it.

Don't offer excuses. Your customer wants a resolution, not an excuse.

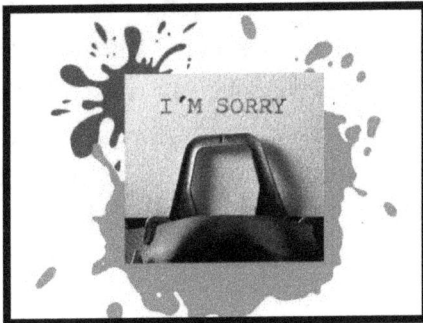

That's what I wanted when a teller at my business bank made a mistake and would not apologize. When I didn't receive a sincere apology, I moved all my accounts to a competing bank.

I had chosen this mid-sized bank many years before because it catered to small businesses, offered personal service, and had convenient locations. One afternoon I was rushing to a three o'clock meeting before heading to the airport for a business trip. On the way, I made what I hoped would be a quick stop to cash a check at the drive-through window at my bank.

I was delighted that there were no other cars in line ahead of me. Yet I waited several minutes and pushed the call button several times before the teller finally showed up at the window. She pushed out the drawer for my transaction, making no apology for keeping me waiting. She couldn't even force a smile or warm greeting.

The teller disappeared with my check and identification for what seemed like forever. When she returned, she plopped the cash, license, and receipt into the drawer and pushed it out to my car. She did not count the cash in front of me as tellers customarily do. She pulled another disappearing act the instant she retracted the drawer.

Before driving away, I counted the money she'd given me and discovered she had given me $100 less than the amount of my check. She appeared agitated when I called her back to the window. She insisted she had given me the correct amount. She got the same count I did when I handed back the stack of hundred dollar bills she'd given me, but she insisted she hadn't made a mistake. She said maybe the $100 bill was somewhere in my car. I would have to wait until after 4:00 when she closed out her drawer for the day to see who was right. Needing to get to my 3:00 appointment, I couldn't wait. I asked for the manager who gave me the same response. Apparently, their tellers never make mistakes.

I was furious that she wouldn't give me the money knowing that if her drawer turned up short, they could deduct the money from one of my accounts. I was exasperated as I left my business card and phone number behind and headed to my meeting.

The voice message from the manager, which I retrieved after my meeting, said the $100 was still in the teller's drawer. They would deposit the money into my account. She begrudgingly added a half-hearted apology **for my inconvenience** without apologizing for their mistake. Then she attempted to excuse the teller's mistake, making the situation even worse. The disagreeable teller didn't even have the courtesy to call and apologize to me herself.

Two weeks later, after opening accounts at a competing bank, I marched into the bank and closed all three accounts. The account representative listened to my story and apologized profusely. Even after her sincere apology, there was nothing she could do to change my mind.

During a few minutes and one abysmal interaction, the *#1 employee in the Sales Prevention Department* had obliterated the goodwill the bank had built up with me over the many years I banked with them when I received great service. This one incident sent me to their competitor.

Anyone can make a mistake, but the way the teller and manager treated me after I pointed out the mistake was rude and inexcusable. If I had not been a long-time customer or if I had not had a sufficient amount of money in my accounts to cover the $100, I might have seen their side—but not their attitude. Their failure to follow their own best practices (counting the money into the drawer in front of me), their unwillingness to agree to a common-sense solution, plus their surly attitude that I must be the one who was in error, told me these were not people I wanted to do business with anymore. I didn't leave the bank because of their fees or location or any of the things you think usually drives someone to the competition. **I left because of the way I was treated.**

I'm not the only one who believes in taking my business where I feel valued and heard. Even when customers love your company or your product, 59% will walk away after several bad experiences, and 17% are gone after just one. You don't have time to get it right. You need to get it right the first time, every time.

An effective and sincere apology can go a long way to heal a bad experience for a customer. Consider using statements such as:

- "I apologize for the mistake. Let me make it right."
- "I'm so sorry you've been inconvenienced," or own the mistake by saying, "I'm so sorry we've inconvenienced you."
- "I'm sorry this has caused you frustration. I will do everything I can to resolve this issue quickly."

It's important to admit mistakes and oversights even if you weren't the person who made the mistake. Customer service requires teamwork. Recognize that you are part of the team and **accept responsibility for the team**. Don't badmouth or criticize another team member. Instead, let your customer know you're truly sorry they are experiencing a problem, and FIX IT.

If you think that the problem was caused by the

customer, you can still tell them you're sorry they're experiencing this problem. This isn't a court of law, and you don't have to prove your innocence. Your goal is to make your customer happy. Figure out what went wrong, educate your customer nicely, and resolve their issue to everyone's satisfaction.

When something goes wrong, your customer's emotions range from a spark of unhappiness to raging anger. It's hard to remain positive and polite with an angry customer, but that is often what it takes to deliver exceptional customer service. If you get defensive or try to avoid responsibility by saying things such as, "It's not my fault," you'll inflame the situation.

What can I do to make it right?

Don't focus on your own inconvenience. In fact, don't even mention it. Remember, it's not about you, it's about the customer you are there to serve.

Timely follow-up is essential to ensure your customer is satisfied. Send them a handwritten note. Even a sincere, personalized email is a simple and effective way to touch base after you've resolved the issue. So few companies follow up that you will stand out when you do. If your customer responds that they still have questions or concerns, your rapid reply will prevent simmering discontent from flaring up.

Your customer is more likely to calm down and accept that mistakes happen if you sincerely apologize, fix the problem quickly, make sure they are happy with the solution, do something extra— even a little something—to compensate them for their inconvenience and follow up when you say you're going to. That's the kind of service that will keep your business growing even when things go wrong.

#7

VALUE CUSTOMER COMPLAINTS

Nobody wants to be confronted by an unhappy customer. But the absence of negative feedback does not indicate your customers are satisfied with your product or service.

What damages a business is not complaints, it's the silent, unhappy customer. The customer who simply walks out of your business or hangs up the phone without letting anyone know they're unhappy. You won't see or hear from them again. A recent survey of 15,000 consumers shows that one-third of the people who have **only one bad experience** will switch to a competitor.

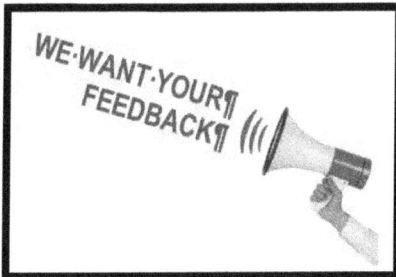

Only one out of 26 unhappy customers let you know they're unhappy. Though most won't tell you what's wrong when they leave, unhappy customers will tell 15 people about their experience. These silent complainers have friends. Their friends have friends. They talk to each other and they post to their social media page—or yours—where their complaints will reach hundreds, maybe thousands of people, not just a few they tell in person. Unless you hear from an unhappy customer directly, you don't have a chance to fix the problem before they damage your business reputation.

I was one of those silently unhappy customers several years ago. When the medical assistants escorted me into an examination room during my frequent visits to my chiropractor, they complained to me about the doctor and his wife and how the practice was run. I listened politely for much too long, but soon wearied of being an unpaid therapist for these women. This doctor wasn't a client, and it was not my place to tell them how to run their business. I felt so uncomfortable after a few months of listening to the office politics that I found another chiropractor. The last time I was there, I said I'd call for my next appointment—and I never did. I was worn out from listening to these stories and didn't care enough to tell the doctor. I didn't want to continue seeing this doctor, so I left without telling any of them why I was leaving. I doubt I was the only one who tired of this toxic environment.

It's important to recognize the immense gift it is when your customer comes to you with complaints. When you know what's wrong, you have the opportunity to fix the problem, keep this customer coming back, and prevent similar problems from driving away other customers. Value those few customers who care enough about doing business with you to let you know they've had a bad experience. Those are the customers who want to do business with you and who will remain loyal if you handle their complaints effectively.

Actively seek out feedback and demonstrate that you're applying what you learn from that feedback. Let your customer know you're making changes. That will positively impact your customers' perspective of your business.

Here's why it's vitally important to listen to and learn from complaints:

- Ninety percent of dissatisfied customers who don't complain directly to the business just leave, so you won't know that something is wrong. If you don't know there's a problem, you can't fix it.

- Those dissatisfied customers simply won't come back. They'll spend their money elsewhere, and you won't even know why you're losing customers.

- The typical unhappy consumer will tell a dozen or more people about their negative experience, and then post the complaint on social media for all their friends and followers to see—and share—again and again.

- If a complaint is resolved quickly, 90% of the time your customer will continue to do business with you. You have a better chance of turning them into a loyal customer if you handle the complaint effectively and resolve the issue to their satisfaction.

- Brands are viewed more favorably by customers when they solicit feedback and use it to better serve their customers.

High-performing businesses take advantage of feedback from customers twice as often as lower-performing companies. When you provide employee training that is focused on customer engagement and satisfaction, you will happily notice the difference in your bottom line.

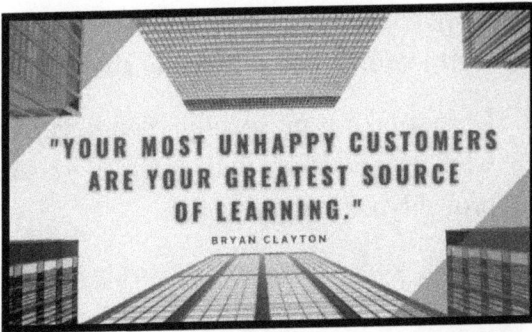

"YOUR MOST UNHAPPY CUSTOMERS ARE YOUR GREATEST SOURCE OF LEARNING."

BRYAN CLAYTON

Take these simple and effective steps when you receive the gift of feedback from your customer:

- Actively listen to what they are saying. Ask questions for clarification. Make sure you understand the complaint and what they want. Do not assume.

- Be proactive in finding a solution.

- Explain what you will do to solve the problem and why. Make sure this solution is acceptable to your customer.

- Handle the complaint quickly and efficiently during the **first** interaction with your customer. You can prevent customers from leaving if you resolve the issue the first time it occurs.

- Offer something to make up for your customer's inconvenience.

- Be polite and respectful no matter what they say to you, but don't tolerate abuse.

- Do not take it personally. You never know what is going on with another person. It probably isn't about you.

- Thank your customer for caring enough to bring the problem to your attention.

- Keep track of complaints. Notice if there's a pattern. If it is a valid complaint, determine how you can proactively address the problem so it doesn't keep happening. Use what you learn from the feedback to make sure your service keeps improving.

Remember, no amount of advertising can repair the damage done by failing to properly address your customer's complaint. If you're not taking care of your customer's complaints, your competition will take care of your customer.

When you recognize that complaints aren't failure, only feedback, you will welcome them and use them to make your service even better.

FINAL THOUGHTS

As a woman who pushes limits, you know how important it is to stand out in your business. You have a valuable service and outstanding products. Your prices are competitive. That alone won't bring you the success that ambitious women like you want and deserve.

Recognize that the majority of people who stop doing business with a company do so because of poor customer experiences. Don't give your customers a reason to leave.

Many people believe customer service is simply a matter of common sense. While providing exceptional service may *appear* easy, it takes outstanding people skills to get it *just right*. Fortunately, these are skills you and your team can learn and further develop. I've seen so many positive changes in my clients' businesses when they implement the strategies I teach.

Build your business by delivering your unique brand

of exceptional service. Put your personal touch on everything you do, and let your customers know you truly care about them.

Always remember that no matter what business you're in, **you're in the customer service business.**

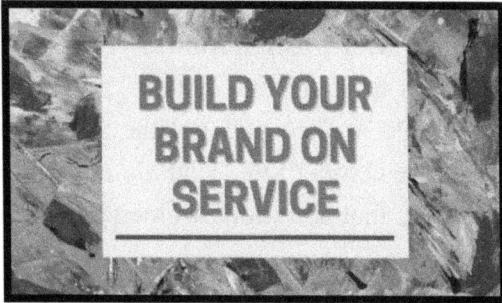

BUILD YOUR
BRAND ON
SERVICE

REFERENCES

Introduction:

"Six Tips to Creating Better Customer Service Loyalty," supperoffice.com, updated 5 January, 2021.

"How to Create A Customer-Centric Strategy for Your Business," superoffice.com, updated 2 March, 2021.

"The Number 1 Reason Why Customers Stay or Leave," customerexperienceinsight.com, June 10, 2013.

"New CX for a New World," zendesk.com.

"Spotlight on CX: The Digital Experience Imperative," zendesk.com.

"How to Be More Empathetic," The *New York Times*, Claire Cain Miller.

Key #1:
"The Role of Customer Experience (Facts, Figures, Tips & More," Matthew DeCarlo, getvoip.com, May 22, 2019.

Key #4:
"Nailing the Job Interview: Make Yourself Memorable," Michael mercer, Ph.D., biospace.com, 12-05-13.

Key #6:
"Experience is everything. Get it right." pwc.com

"37 Customer Experience Statistics You Need to Know for 2021," Toma Kulbyte, superoffice.com, 24 March, 2021.

Key #7:
"50 Important Customer Experience Stats for Busines Leaders," Vala Afshar, *Huffington Post*, December 6, 2017.

"100 Essential Customer Service Statistics and Trends for 2021," nextiva.com, updated May 10, 2020.

"Customer Experience for Executives," slideshare.net, September 3, 2015.

ABOUT THE AUTHOR

Lynn W. Murphy, M.Ed., is a speaker, author, and leadership development expert who works with organizations and success-minded individuals who want to accelerate their performance and more quickly achieve their goals by mastering interpersonal skills and team dynamics. She is the president and founder of Key Innovative Business Solutions.

You may have seen Lynn sharing customer service tips on the Fox 10 Phoenix morning show. She has worked with organizations such as Marriott International, US Bureau of Land Management, and Ford Motor Company.

Inspired by the many remarkable women who are claiming leadership roles in business and politics, she created the *Women Who Push the Limits* movement to inspire, motivate, and empower women to claim their power. For her soon-to-be published book by the same name, Lynn has gathered stories from remarkable women who have created success in spite of, or because of, the challenges they've had in their lives. Through these stories you'll learn to find your voice, speak your truth, and change the world by owning your power.

Stay connected with Lynn:

- Visit Lynn's website for more information on her speaking, coaching, and training programs:
  KeyInnovativeBusinessSolutions.com

- Like **Key Innovative Business Solutions** on Facebook.

- Visit **womenwhopushthelimits.com** where you can join our mailing list. You'll be the first to learn about the release date for the book *Women Who Push the Limits* and upcoming events for this community.

- Like **Women Who Push the Limits** on Facebook.

Find your voice. Speak your truth. Change the world.

Lynn W. Murphy, M.Ed.
Speaker, Author, and Founder of
Women Who Push the Limits

Women WHO PUSH THE LIMITS